32

# ★ IT'S MY STATE! ★

# Vermont

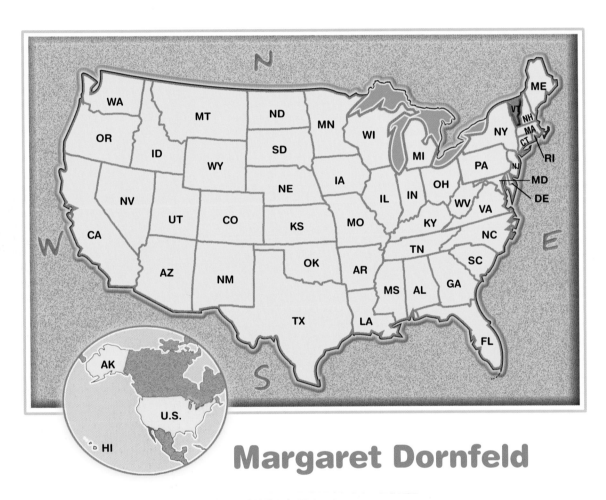

## Margaret Dornfeld

 **Marshall Cavendish**
Benchmark
New York

Series Consultant

*David G. Vanderstel, Ph.D., Executive Director, National Council on Public History*

*With thanks to Amy Cunningham, Director of Education, Vermont Historical Society, for her expert review of the manuscript.*

Marshall Cavendish Benchmark
99 White Plains Road
Tarrytown, New York 10591-9001
www.marshallcavendish.us

Maps, text, and illustrations copyright © 2005 by Marshall Cavendish Corporation
Maps and illustrations by Chris Santoro

Library of Congress Cataloging-in-Publication Data

Dornfeld, Margaret.
Vermont / by Margaret Dornfeld.
p. cm. -- (It's my state!)
Includes index.
ISBN 0-7614-1864-4
1. Vermont--Juvenile literature. I. Title. II. Series.

F49.3.D67 2005
974.3--dc22

2004022734

Photo research by Candlepants, Inc.

Cover photograph: Mike Brison/Getty Images

Back cover: The license plate shows Vermont's postal abbreviation, followed by its year of statehood.

The photographs in this book are used by permission and through the courtesy of:
*Corbis:* 14, 21, 22, 34, 35; Kit Houghton, 4 (top); Clive Druett/Papilo, 4 (middle); David Aubrey, 5 (top); Robert Estall, 5 (middle); David Muench, 9; Phil Schermeister,10; Peter Finger, 11; James P. Blair, 12, 36, 52, 69; Michael Maconachie, 18 (middle); Kennan Ward, 18 (bottom); Robert T. Nowitz, 38; Joseph Sohm/Visions of America, 40; David H. Wells, 41; Kelly-Mooney Photography, 45; Bettmann, 28, 29, 42 (bottom), 43 (top), 44 (bottom); Pellicier Micheline, 43 (middle); Paul Thompson/Ecoscene, 64; Darrell Gulin, 66; Ron Watts, 73; Becky Luigart-Stayner, 70 (top); Joseph Sohm/Chromosohm Inc., 70 (middle); Randy M. Ury, 71 (middle); Duomo, 71 (bottom). *Photo Researchers Inc.:* Gail Jankus, 4 (bottom); Rod Planck, 5 (bottom); Jim Zipp, 19 (middle); Ken Thomas, 19 (bottom); A. Hart-Davis, 71 (top).*The Image Works:* Townsend P. Dickinson, 8; Rob Crandell, 13; Lee Snider, 54; Joe Sohm, 57, 70 (bottom); Alden Pellet, 60. Minden Pictures: Tim Fitzharris, 16; Tom Vezo, 17. *Index Stock Imagery:* John Warden,18 (top); Mark Hunt, 48; Barry Winiker, 49; Kindra Clineff, 51; Dennis Curren, 53, 65, 68. *Envision:* Jean Higgins, 19 (top); George Mattei, 67. *North Wind Picture Archive:* 25, 26, 37 (top). *Vermont Historical Society:* 31, 32, 33. *Getty Images:* TimeLife Pictures/ Terry Ashe, 37 (bottom); TimeLife Pictures, 42 (top); Steve Liss, 42(middle); Brooke Slezak, 62.

Series design by Anahid Hamparian
Printed in Italy

1 3 5 6 4 2

# Contents

# A Quick Look at Vermont

**Nickname:** The Green Mountain State
**Population:** 619,107 (2003 estimate)
**Statehood:** March 4, 1791

## Animal: Morgan Horse

*In 1791 a Vermont teacher named Justin Morgan became the owner of a young stallion named Figure. The horse was small, but became famous for its strength and speed. The horse became the father of a new breed, the Morgan, still known for its athletic ability.*

## Bird: Hermit Thrush

*With its brown back and speckled breast, the hermit thrush can be hard to spot in the Vermont woods. It is better known for its flutelike song, which can be heard on summer days from just before dawn to sunset.*

## Flower: Red Clover

*A common sight along country roads, red clover is a reminder of Vermont's farming heritage. Experts say that the red clover is actually not even a native plant. Hundreds of years ago, European settlers brought the flower to the region that now includes Vermont.*

## Butterfly: Monarch

*A fifth-grade class in Cornwall chose the monarch as the state butterfly in 1987. The students said its colors recall many sides of Vermont: orange for autumn leaves, black for soil, white for snow, and yellow for fields of dandelions.*

## Tree: Sugar Maple

*Native Americans who lived in the region taught European settlers how best to get sap from the sugar maples. As a result, Vermonters have been collecting sap—or tapping the trees—for hundreds of years. The sap is boiled to make syrup. It takes about forty gallons of sap to make a gallon of pure maple syrup.*

## Amphibian: Northern Leopard Frog

*The northern leopard frog lives around Vermont's ponds and wetlands. It has green or brown skin and spots throughout its body. These frogs are sometimes called meadow frogs or grass frogs. Lawmakers made it a state symbol in 1997 as a reminder to keep waterways healthy.*

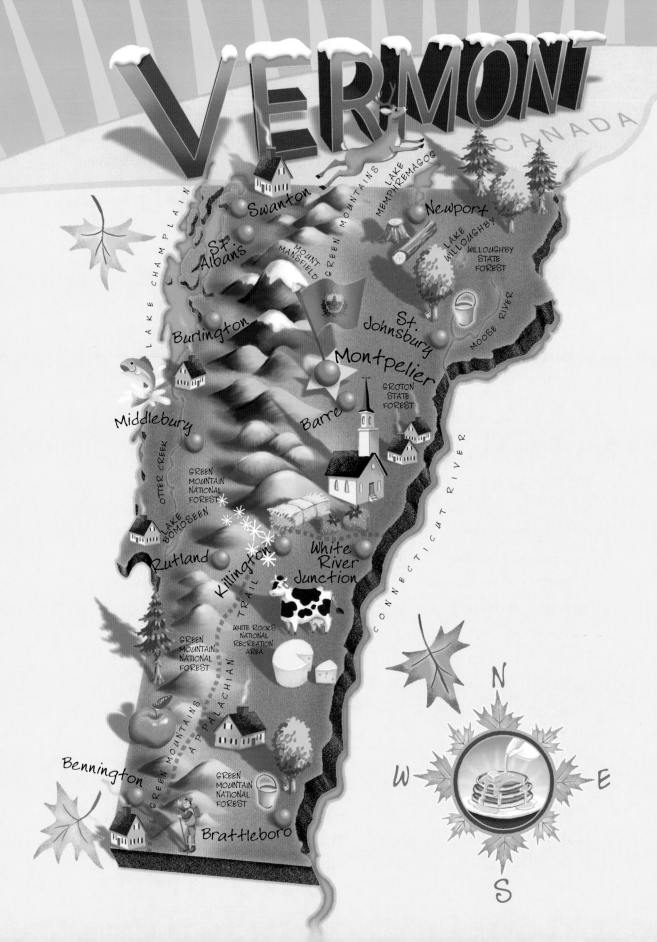

# 1 The Green Mountain State

Vermont can mean quiet woods, deep snow, or glittering water. It can mean a winding road, a white church, and an old-fashioned country store. But more than anything else, Vermont means mountains.

The Green Mountains spread the length of Vermont, shaping almost everything that happens there. The mountains light up with color in autumn. In winter, they cast evening shadows over snow-covered hills. They feed rivers and streams that help keep the state green. Vermont is known as the Green Mountain State, and when you travel through it, a lovely view seems to be around every corner. As one writer put it, "you drink up beauty like rich milk" wherever you turn.

## Vermont's Borders
**North: Canada**
**South: Massachusetts**
**East: New Hampshire**
**West: New York**

## Mountains and Valleys

Vermont sits up near the northeastern corner of the United States, in a part of the country called New England. (New England is made up of six states in the northeastern part of the

*A view of the Deerfield River Valley in southern Vermont. Haystack Mountain can be seen in the distance.*

country: Connecticut, Maine, Massachusetts, New Hampshire, Rhode Island, and Vermont.) Vermont is a small state, about 160 miles long and 80 miles wide. But some people say if Vermont's wrinkled mountains and valleys were ironed flat, the state would spread as wide as Texas. That is almost thirty times larger than Vermont's present area.

The Green Mountains run like a backbone down the center of Vermont, and are covered with a thick blanket of trees. The highest peak, Mount Mansfield, juts up 4,393 feet, making it the highest point in the state. But like other Vermont mountains, the Green Mountains were once much taller than this. The stone that makes up the Green Mountains has been worn down over millions of years. During the Ice Age, about 10,000

*Mount Mansfield, located along the Green Mountains, is the highest point in Vermont.*

years ago, thick sheets of slow-moving ice called glaciers scraped across the mountains. As the glaciers moved, they changed land features and brought huge amounts of sand, soil, and rock. Vermont still has huge rocks that were carried and left behind by the glaciers. One of the largest, called the Green Mountain Giant, sits in the southern part of the state. This boulder is 25 feet high, 40 feet long, and 125 feet around.

Many peaks in the Green Mountains are big enough to have names. A hiking path called the Long Trail runs from one peak to another. The trail stretches 270 miles, from the top of Vermont to the Massachusetts border. Shady forests, cool waterfalls, and dazzling views mark the way.

*I have found the Vermont hills easier and happier to live in than the Rocky Mountains or even the Alps.*
—author Sinclair Lewis

To the east of the Green Mountains lies the Connecticut River Valley, an area of quiet towns, woods, and green rolling hills. The Connecticut River forms the border between Vermont and New Hampshire. The river flows gently south toward the bottom of New England. Smaller rivers, such as the White and West rivers, spill down the Green Mountains into the Connecticut, rushing and swirling when the snow melts in spring.

*Many Vermont farms are located on the fertile land along the shores of the Connecticut River.*

*Cool water rushes down a waterfall at Moss Glen Falls near Stowe.*

Another valley spreads to the west of the Green Mountains, around a long, deep body of water called Lake Champlain. The lake stretches about half the length of the state, along the Vermont–New York border. It is fed by the Missisquoi, Lamoille, and Winooski rivers and Otter Creek. Around the lake, dairy cows graze on some of Vermont's richest farmland. The state's biggest city, Burlington, hugs the lakeshore.

North of Burlington, a group of islands cluster in Lake Champlain. Native American, French, and British families lived there at different times in the state's history. Today the largest islands are dotted with summer cottages and farms.

*The city of Burlington is situated on the shore of Lake Champlain.*

**Vermont**

## Climate

Vermont summers are usually mild, with warm days and cool nights. Morning mists often rise in the valleys, then dissolve into a clear blue sky.

> *The night was as keen as the edge of a newly-ground sword; breath froze on the coat-lapels in snow; the nose became without sensation, and the eyes wept bitterly . . .*
>
> —author Rudyard Kipling, on his first visit to Brattleboro

The average temperature during the summer is about 68 degrees Fahrenheit. Once in a while a heat wave strikes. The hottest Vermont day ever recorded was July 4, 1911, in Vernon, where the thermometer hit 105 degrees.

Autumn and winter can bring crisp, clear days, as well as wet weather. By January, the state is usually covered with a thick blanket of snow. Temperatures drop below freezing, and icy winds chill the air even more. Vermont winters can be long and frigid. The average winter temperature is 17 degrees. The coldest recorded day was December 30, 1933, in Bloomfield, when the temperature plunged to -50 degrees. Every year, Vermont receives about 40 inches of precipitation—melted snow, rain, and other moisture. The mountainous areas in the state receive the most snow—an average of 80 to 120 inches each year. The Connecticut River and Champlain valleys receive less, averaging about 70 inches per year.

*A family uses their toboggan to enjoy Vermont's wintry weather.*

Around March, the ice and snow begin melting. But it takes weeks for spring to really arrive. Snow turns to slush, and tires sink into the muck on mountain roads. Vermonters call this period mud season. It is the one time of year many Vermonters prefer to stay inside.

## Forests and Fields

Large areas of the Vermont forest were once cleared for farming. The woods have grown back, but in many places, old stone walls from the farms can still be seen among the trees. A few areas, such as Mount Mansfield State Forest, have maple and beech trees up to 200 years old.

Today about three-quarters of Vermont is covered with forests. The state has more than one hundred kinds of trees. Vermont's evergreens include hemlock, spruce, pine, and cedar. Beside them grow trees that start to lose their leaves in the fall. These include ash, elm, birch, maple, beech, and poplar.

When autumn comes, it sets the woods glowing with brilliant colors. Beeches, ashes, and hickories turn different shades of yellow. Sugar maples turn amber, gold, and scarlet. Vermont's fall leaves are so bright that tourists come from around the United States and many other countries to catch

*In the fall, the leaves of many of Vermont's trees change to bright red, orange, or yellow.*

*The woods are lovely, dark and deep,*
*But I have promises to keep,*
*And miles to go before I sleep.*

**—from a poem written by Robert Frost at**
**Shaftsbury, Vermont**

the display. Each year the amount of color is a little bit different. Sunny fall days with cool nights help the leaves turn brightest. Fall color reports in newspapers and on the Internet—a little like weather reports—help "leaf-peepers" (people who enjoy seeing the bright fall colors) hit the best spots.

Trees are bare and trimmed with snow for months during winter. But just before the first buds of spring appear, the sap of sugar maples starts flowing. Vermonters tap the trees at around this time and boil the sweet liquid down to make maple syrup.

In spring and summer, delicate wildflowers bloom in the Vermont woods. White, yellow, and purple violets cluster between the roots of trees. Irises grow on the banks of streams, and bog laurel crowds mountain marshes. In September, swaying goldenrods and purple asters fill Vermont meadows.

Vermont also has flowering plants that are very rare. One simple plant called Jesup's milk-vetch grows only a few places in the United States. This bluish-purple flower is a member of the pea family. It clings to the thin soil on rocks along the Connecticut River near Hartland. Jesup's milk-vetch is an endangered plant, so people are not allowed to pick it, even if they own the land it grows on. State planners must also think carefully before threatening its home with major changes, such as a dam that would cause the river level to rise.

## Running Wild

The Vermont woods are rich in wildlife. Chipmunks dart between rocks, around trees, and over logs. Many other forest animals sleep during the day and are not usually seen until late afternoon or evening. White-tailed deer may nibble green twigs at sunset, and moose wade through rivers in the northeast woods. Beavers swim out from their lodges to chew on aspen trees. Rabbits leave their burrows to look for food. So do predators such as bobcats, mink, and foxes.

The cool lakes and rivers of the Green Mountain State are filled with fish and other animals that live underwater. Large fish, such as landlocked salmon and northern pike, and small ones, such as smelt, share the deep waters of Lake Champlain.

*A large male moose walks across parts of a lake in search of food.*

*A belted kingfisher perches on a branch as it eats the small fish it has caught.*

Perch, trout, and bass live in rivers and streams. Many birds that live near the water, such as herons, egrets, kingfishers, and osprey, depend on the fish for food.

Two hundred years ago, the catamount—also called the cougar, panther, puma, or mountain lion—roamed the Green Mountains. This big cat, with its wild grace, once stood for the freedom of the Vermont frontier. But as farmers and loggers cleared acres of forests, they destroyed the catamount's natural home. Hunters and trappers killed animals the big cats needed for food, as well as the cats themselves. By the 1960s, mountain lions had died out in Vermont, and most of the eastern United States.

But even though they are officially extinct, hundreds of people have reported seeing cougars in Vermont in the past thirty years. So far, no one has been able to prove Vermont has living mountain lions. But if the big cats do make a comeback, the remote woods of the northern part of the state might be a likely place for them to make their home.

# Plants & Animals

### Red Maple

The red maple, also called the swamp maple, is one of the jewels of the Vermont woods. In early fall, when most leaves are still green, the red maple turns flaming crimson. Its sudden splashes of fiery color can take your breath away.

### Wood Sorrel

Each May, delicate wood sorrel blooms in the shade of Vermont forests. Its cloverlike leaves fold up at night and in stormy weather. The leaves were once used in salads and as medicine. The word sorrel *comes from the French* sur, *which means "sour."*

### Snowshoe Hare

On winter mornings, the Vermont woods are often criss-crossed with the tracks of snowshoe hares. These animals change color with the seasons. They gradually replace their brown summer coat with white fur to match the winter snow. Snowshoe hares are also speedy. They may run as fast as 28 miles an hour to escape a fox or an owl.

## Wild Turkey

*In the 1800s, Vermonters cut down so many trees that some woodland animals, including the wild turkey, disappeared from the state. But about thirty years ago, biologists brought wild turkeys back to Vermont. The birds now nest again in the Green Mountains, where they feed on the nuts of oak, beech, and hickory trees.*

## Spring Peeper

*The tiny frogs called spring peepers are easier to hear than they are to see. They perch on the grasses that grow near ponds and wetlands and loudly peep to find mates in spring. An adult spring peeper may measure less than an inch but can jump half a yard to get away from enemies.*

## Chickadee

*Black-capped chickadees live in Vermont all seasons of the year. They often form small flocks and hop between branches of evergreen trees. When threatened by an intruder, a chickadee warns other birds with its familiar call of "chick-a-dee-dee-dee."*

## Cleaning Up

Vermont is one of the leading states when it comes to protecting the environment. But one challenge it still faces is how to keep water life healthy. Lakes and ponds are especially threatened by phosphorus, a chemical that gets washed from farms, cities, and sewage treatment plants into the state's waterways. As phosphorus builds up in lakes, it causes too much algae to grow. The algae can rob other plants and animals of oxygen until they sicken and die. One spot where algae has become a problem is Missisquoi Bay, in northern Lake Champlain.

Vermont citizens have helped the state learn more about this problem by monitoring algae and phosphorus levels at different spots in Lake Champlain. Their research gives scientists a rough idea how much phosphorus is too much. Now the state is taking steps to control the pollution. That may mean using new methods for sewage treatment, a change that could cost millions of dollars. Farmers may also need support from the state to control runoff from manure in fields. But despite cost, in 2003, Governor James Douglas announced plans for a major cleanup. "The earlier we achieve significant pollution reductions," said Douglas, "the sooner our waters can begin to restore themselves."

*Vermont's residents value their state and work hard to keep it clean and beautiful.*

# **2** **From the Beginning**

## The First Residents

Around 8,000 years ago, the land that is now Vermont had wide stretches of open land, and Lake Champlain was a saltwater sea. People camped in small groups along the shores of the sea. They may have caught fish, seals, and shellfish for food. They may also have hunted caribou—animals similar to reindeer that once roamed the land in gigantic herds. No one knows exactly what life was like for these early residents. The only clues they left behind are spear tips and other stone tools found buried in the ground near Lake Champlain.

Little by little, the region grew warmer, and the landscape changed. Forests spread across the hills. People started to lead a different kind of life there. They learned to make pottery from clay. They hunted and fished, but they also gathered food from the forest, such as acorns, hickory nuts, and raspberries. Later on, they learned to grow crops such as beans, squash, and corn.

By around 1600, villages dotted the shores of Lake Champlain and the Connecticut River. They belonged to a Native

*A young girl works at a cotton mill in North Pownal around 1910.*

American group called the Abenaki. The Abenaki lived in structures called wigwams. They were made of wooden frames covered with wide strips of bark from birch, basswood, or elm trees. The Abenaki also used birchbark for canoes and baskets.

For the Abenaki, life changed with the seasons. In winter they paddled upstream to the mountains to hunt moose and deer. When spring was on its way, they collected sap from sugar maple trees and made maple syrup. In summer and fall they tended their fields and gathered wild plants to make medicine. They dried meat, fish, berries, and corn to eat when the weather turned cold.

## Newcomers Arrive

In July 1609, a band of Native American warriors from northern regions paddled into the great lake the Abenaki called Bitawbagok. Three white men were with them. The leader of the whites was a French explorer named Samuel de Champlain.

The war party and Europeans came face to face with their enemy, the Iroquois—a Native American group that was also living in the region that now includes Vermont. Champlain stepped

> *We entered the lake, which is of great extent, say eighty or a hundred leagues long, where I saw four fine islands. . . . There are also many rivers falling into the lake, bordered by many fine trees.*
>
> —explorer Samuel de Champlain

*Champlain used his gun to fight the Iroquois while his Native American allies used bows, arrows, and other traditional weapons.*

forward and fired his gun, killing two Iroquois leaders. The Native Americans with Champlain fought the Iroquois, but many of the Iroquois fled. This was mainly because they had never seen guns before and did not know how to fight these strange men with powerful weapons. Champlain named the lake after himself and claimed the land around it for France. As far as anyone knows, he and his men were the first Europeans to see the body of water now known as Lake Champlain.

The Abenaki were not a part of this battle, and they never met Champlain. But they saw many changes soon after he came. More Frenchmen followed in Champlain's footsteps. These newcomers brought cotton cloth, iron pots, glass beads, and other goods the Abenaki had never used before. The Abenaki also traded with the French for guns and ammunition—weapons that could help them in war.

In 1666 the French built a fort to protect their new territory, on Isle La Motte in Lake Champlain. More French forts and villages sprang up along the lakeshore. On the other side of the Green Mountains, British soldiers and settlers started moving in too. In 1724 they built their first Vermont town, Fort Dummer, on the Connecticut River near what is now Brattleboro.

*A colored woodcut shows early Vermont settlers traveling to the new land along the Connecticut River.*

As Europeans pushed in from both sides, battles broke out all over the land. Between 1689 and 1760, the French and the British fought many times in North America. Native Americans of different groups joined in on both sides.

The French and Indian War lasted from 1754 to 1763. In this war the French and the British were fighting over rights to the land. As in previous battles, Native Americans of the region took different sides. During the war, the Abenaki helped capture more than 1,000 British settlers. They marched their prisoners north through present-day Vermont to lands controlled by France. Some prisoners died on the way, but many lived to tell their stories. They painted a vivid picture of the Natives and the wild country they had traveled through.

But the Native Americans living in the region were greatly affected by the European traders and settlers. As settlements spread, Native American communities were forced to move north toward present-day Canada. They had no choice but to leave the lands their ancestors had occupied for centuries. The Native American population in the region decreased as several Native Americans died during the wars between the French and British. Many others died from diseases brought by the Europeans.

## The Green Mountain Boys

In 1763 the British won control of North America. Even before the French and Indian War ended, British settlers were clearing new land. The royal governor of New Hampshire, Benning Wentworth, sold many pieces of land—known as grants—in the area just to the west of the Green Mountains. By 1770 hundreds of people from Massachusetts and Connecticut had settled in the New Hampshire grants.

But the settlers had a problem: according to the British king, the land really belonged to New York. New York officials kept trying to make the settlers leave or pay rent on their farms. The settlers refused. Instead, they teamed up to defend the property they believed was rightfully theirs. They elected a leader named Ethan Allen, a proud, quick-witted man who knew the Green Mountains well.

*Ethan Allen was born in Connecticut in 1738 and died in Vermont in 1789.*

Allen went to a court in Albany, New York, to prove the settlers were right, but the judge rejected his argument. Allen was furious. "The gods of the hills are not the gods of the valley," he announced. With these strange words of warning, he rode back to protect the land by force.

Allen gathered about 200 men to fight for the New Hampshire grants. They called themselves the Green Mountain Boys. Instead of wearing uniforms like a regular army, they wore evergreen twigs in their caps. When New Yorkers came near the New Hampshire grants, the Green Mountain Boys ambushed them and drove them away.

## A New Republic

At first, New Yorkers called the Green Mountain Boys "rioters and traitors." But in 1775, when the colonies began fighting for independence from Great Britain, the Green Mountain Boys were an important part of the patriot cause. Soon after the first shots of the Revolutionary War rang out, the Green Mountain Boys captured Fort Ticonderoga, a British post in New York territory. When New York leaders found out, they actually paid Allen and his men and bought them uniforms.

Most settlers in the New Hampshire grants believed in the Revolution. But they still did not believe in submitting to New York, or to any of the other thirteen colonies. So in 1777, at a meeting in the town of Westminster, they decided to form a nation of their own. Borrowing the French words for green mountain—*vert mont*—they named the new nation the Republic of Vermont.

Vermont leaders signed a bold constitution at Windsor in 1777. It was the first to make slavery illegal. It also gave all men over twenty-one the right to vote. That was an unusual rule at the time. In other states, voters had to be men who owned land. In 1778 Vermonters elected a group of representatives called the Vermont Assembly.

For years Vermont continued to be independent. But it had to fight to survive. The British and their Native American allies raided many Vermont towns during the Revolutionary War. But the Green Mountain Boys and other Vermonters beat them back during the Battle of Bennington in 1777.

*General John Stark led the victorious American troops at the Battle of Bennington.*

## The Fourteenth State

The Revolutionary War ended in 1783. With the country at peace, Vermont's population climbed. By 1785 Vermont had its own newspaper and post offices. The tiny republic even issued its own copper coins.

In 1790 New York and Vermont finally came to an agreement. Vermont promised to pay New York $30,000 to put old arguments to rest. In 1791 the Vermont Assembly voted 105 to 2 to adopt the U.S. Constitution. That same year, every member of the U.S. Congress voted to accept Vermont as the fourteenth state.

Vermont had about 85,000 people when it joined the Union—almost three times as many as when the republic was formed. Over the next twenty years, it became the nation's fastest-growing state. New settlers cleared land for farming. They built sawmills along streams, and dug canals to help boats carry goods between towns.

The settlers did not have an easy life. Farming the rocky soil of the Green Mountains was backbreaking work. Some years, heavy rainstorms made streams overflow and wash away bridges and barns. Other years saw almost no rain at all. A young boy named Elias Smith moved with his family from Connecticut to Woodstock in 1782. They walked 180 miles to get to their new home. "I was disappointed, grieved, vexed [irritated], and mad," Elias wrote in his diary after seeing the place. "Though I was some over thirteen years, I cried."

## Building a Future

Vermonters kept looking for new ways to bring wealth to the state. They started raising sheep during the War of 1812, when the country needed wool. By 1840 Vermont had six times as many sheep as people. Some farmers got rich from the wool trade. But in the 1850s, when sheep farming spread to the western states, Vermont sheep farmers could not compete. Vermont had to find another way to succeed.

The first postage stamp used in the United States was made in Brattleboro in 1846.

Even during hard times, the state continued to make its voice heard. In the mid-1800s, Vermont fought to end slavery in the American South. Its citizens helped runaway slaves get to Canada by giving them shelter along a secret route to the North called the Underground Railroad. The state also passed laws to keep slaveowners from taking runaways back.

In 1861 the Civil War broke out between the North and South. Vermont was the first state to offer troops to the North. About 35,000 Vermont men fought in the war. About 10,000 were killed or disabled. The war ended in 1865. With so many losses, it was a difficult time in Vermont, and many people left to try their luck in other parts of the country.

*Taken around 1861, this photograph shows the Third Vermont Regiment at Camp Baxter in St. Johnsbury, Vermont. Vermont soldiers fought on the side of the North, which was also called the Union.*

Some Vermonters who stayed earned their living raising dairy cows. Others found work in Burlington lumber mills. Once railroads were built to help transport heavy goods, Vermont became a national center for granite and marble. Some of these businesses brought workers from other parts of the world. Scottish, Spanish, and Italians cut and carved granite in Barre. People from Poland, Spain, Greece, and Russia worked for the Vermont Marble Company in Proctor.

*Teams of horses were used to pull granite that was mined from Vermont's quarries. This photograph was taken in the early 1900s.*

*Throughout the twentieth century, Vermont's cities continued to grow. Here, the state capital, Montpelier, is shown with cars lined up along Main Street.*

## New Vermont

In the twentieth century, Vermont dairy farms became famous for their milk, cheese, and butter. The state also began to attract summer visitors, who paid well for the chance to hunt, fish, or taste country life by waking up on a farm. But the state's rocky soil, steep hillsides, and bitter cold still made it a tough place to earn a living.

*A dairy farmer strains milk at his farm in Kirby.*

**Vermont**

It was not until the 1930s that Vermonters learned to make the most of their steep slopes and snowstorms. When Americans took up skiing, Vermonters realized they had "white gold." The first ski lift in the United States was built in Woodstock in 1934. The simple towrope got its power from the engine of a Ford Model T automobile. Six years later the nation's first chairlift started carrying skiers in Stowe.

Vermont became better known as a vacation spot, thanks to the ski season. Many skiers came back in summer and fell in love with the quiet, unspoiled land. By the 1960s, people who wanted to escape from the cities thought of Vermont as a great place to start new lives. Young men and women who wanted to get closer to nature started farms in Vermont and did their best to live off the land. Vacation houses popped up in the mountains and around lakes. Many writers and artists also moved in.

*In 1947, these skiers enjoyed the slopes at the Bromley Resort in southern Vermont.*

Today, Vermont has a lot more people than it did in the 1950s—about 50 percent more. The state has more buildings, more traffic, and more roads as well. Yet it also has more laws to protect the environment. In 1970 Vermont passed the Environmental Control Law (also known as Act 250), which lets the state limit development. Since then, the government has taken many other steps to protect Vermont's land, air, and waterways. One example is Green-Up Day which is held each year on the first Saturday in May. A tradition since about 1970, Vermont children take the day to become involved in keeping the Vermont landscape beautiful. Many Vermonters believe steps like these are the key to the future. As long as the state keeps its natural beauty, it will always have something wonderful to give.

*Residents of Bristol gather for a Fourth of July parade through town. Through the years, Vermonters have continued to participate in festivals and celebrations that honor the state's history and keep traditions alive.*

# Important Dates

**8000–1000 B.C.E.** Early residents live near Lake Champlain.

**1000 B.C.E.–1600 C.E.** Native Americans living in the region that now includes Vermont learn to raise crops and hunt with bows and arrows.

**1609** Samuel de Champlain enters Lake Champlain and claims the land around it for France.

**1666** French soldiers build a fort on Isle La Motte, creating Vermont's first white settlement.

**1724** British troops build Fort Dummer at Dummerston.

**1749** Governor Benning Wentworth makes the first New Hampshire grant, for the town of Bennington.

**1770** The Green Mountain Boys team up to protect the New Hampshire grants from New York.

**1777** Vermont declares itself an independent republic.

**1791** Vermont becomes the fourteenth state.

**1840** Vermont has six times as many sheep as people.

**1859** The present capitol, the State House, is built in Montpelier.

**1864** Confederate soldiers raid St. Albans in the northernmost battle of the Civil War.

**1881** Chester A. Arthur of Fairfield becomes U.S. president.

**1923** Calvin Coolidge of Plymouth Notch becomes U.S. president.

**1930** The Vermont population hits 359,611, but cows outnumber people.

**1962** Vermont elects Philip H. Hoff, the state's first Democratic governor since 1853.

**1970** Vermont passes Act 250, the first statewide law to control land use.

**1984** For the first time, Vermont elects a woman governor, Madeleine M. Kunin.

**1997** Vermonter Jody Williams wins the Nobel Peace Prize for leading the fight against land mines.

**2003** Howard Dean, who had served as Vermont's governor for ten years, announces his (ultimately unsuccessful) plan to run for president of the United States.

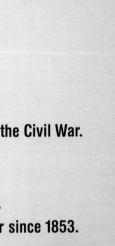

*Samuel de Champlain*

*Madeleine M. Kunin*

# 3 The People

More than 600,000 people live in Vermont today. That is a small number compared to most other states. Vermont is mostly forests, farms, and villages, not big cities. Its heart is in the country, and Vermonters tend to be proud of their ties with the land. They are also known for loving freedom and independence. According to author Dorothy Canfield Fisher, there is an unwritten Vermont law that "everyone must be allowed to do, think, believe whatever seems best to him."

## Living Together

About half of the people who live in Vermont were born in the state. Many have Vermont roots that go back a long way. Dairy farmer Rosina Wallace still works in the fields bought by her great-grandparents in the 1800s. "Farming is tiring and hard work but I grew up on this farm," says Wallace. "I love the view almost as much as scratching a cow behind the ears." Other Vermont families have a long tradition of working in granite quarries or lumber mills.

*Montpelier schoolchildren enjoy delicious Vermont ice cream.*

*Many people move to Vermont because they enjoy living in quiet, historic New England communities like Stowe.*

Many other Vermonters come from other places. In the 1960s and 1970s, young men and women who dreamed of living close to nature found a home in the state. Some started organic farms, raising animals and growing crops without chemical fertilizers or pesticides. Others went into business selling traditional crafts such as handmade furniture or pottery. Sometimes families who took vacations in Vermont simply started living there year round.

Little by little, these newcomers have become as much a part of Vermont as the families who have lived there for generations. Jay Craven is a filmmaker who moved from New York to Vermont in 1974. He makes movies right near his home in St. Johnsbury and enjoys working with small-town communities.

"Vermont has a traditional conservatism," says Craven, "which basically says that for things to change they should change only for good reason. But once the good reason is presented, things do change. There is an openness in Vermont by people to respect all points of view."

*An Indian family living in Burlington practices their Hindu religion. Though they make up a small part of the population, many people from other countries make Vermont their home.*

The population in Vermont is mostly Caucasian, or white. African Americans make up about 0.5 percent, Asians and Asian Americans make up about 0.9 percent, and people of Hispanic or Latino descent represent about 0.9 percent. Before European settlement, the region's entire population was Native American. Today, however, Native Americans represent less than 1 percent of the state population.

Some people moving to Vermont today come from far away places such as Asia or Latin America. They include refugees who came to the United States to escape dangerous political situations. Starting in 2001, a Vermont refugee program brought people from Sudan and Somalia, African countries torn by civil war. Starting life over in a new part of the world is often lonely and difficult, but it can also bring hope. Ibrahim Jafar, from Somalia, brought his family to Winooski, Vermont, in 2003. "We knew only that we were going to a strange land, to a place we never heard of, a city we never heard of," he said during a welcome ceremony at Winooski's city hall. "Already it seems like home."

# Famous Vermonters

### Andrea Mead Lawrence:
### Olympic Skier

*Andrea Mead Lawrence skied into Olympic history when she was just nineteen. Born in Rutland, she hit the slopes at age three, started racing at age ten, and won U.S. championship titles in the 1950s. At the 1952 Olympic games in Oslo, Norway, Lawrence won two gold medals—a first for U.S. women in alpine skiing.*

### Ben Cohen and Jerry Greenfield:
### Ice Cream Makers

*Two friends, Ben Cohen and Jerry Greenfield, decided to go into business together so they could be their own bosses—and have fun. They opened the first Ben & Jerry's ice cream shop in 1978 in a former Burlington gas station. As the company grew, Cohen and Greenfield made sure some of the money it earned went to causes they believed in.*

### Elisha Graves Otis: Inventor

*Born in Halifax, Vermont, Elisha Graves Otis invented the elevator brake. Otis came up with the idea while working at a factory. The company needed a brake for a hoist in order to lift heavy equipment safely. In 1854 Otis demonstrated his new device at a fair in New York City. While riding an elevator, he applied the brake and had the elevator cable cut with an axe. The platform held, proving that people could ride several stories safely.*

## Norman Rockwell: Illustrator

*Norman Rockwell was one of the United States' best-loved illustrators. Born in New York City in 1894, Rockwell lived in Arlington, Vermont, from 1939 to 1953. He captured the small-town life he saw around him in dozens of pictures for the covers of magazines. Rockwell painted simple scenes in loving detail: a family having Thanksgiving dinner, children sledding, or girls getting drinks at a soda fountain. In 1977, he was awarded the Presidential Medal of Freedom.*

## Jody Williams:
## Human Rights Leader

*A native of Brattleboro, Jody Williams is a world leader in the fight against land mines, one of the most deadly weapons used in wars. Land mines are explosives that are planted in the ground. They are often left behind when a war is over, and can kill or cripple people even in peace-time. To stop them, Williams formed a group called the International Campaign to Ban Landmines (ICBL) in the early 1990s. The group has won support from leaders around the globe. In 1997, Williams and the ICBL won one of the world's highest honors: the Nobel Peace Prize.*

## Calvin Coolidge:
## United States President

*Born in Plymouth Notch in 1872, Calvin Coolidge was the thirtieth U.S. president. Coolidge served as vice president starting in 1921. He was visiting his Vermont home when he heard that President Warren G. Harding had died, and that he had to take charge of the nation. Nicknamed Silent Cal, he became famous as a sharp-witted man of few words.*

## Celebrating the Arts

The arts are a big part of life in Vermont. Some of the state's most popular art forms go back to when the state first formed. Others are new and experimental.

In many Vermont towns, dancers still swing their partners to old-time New England fiddle tunes. People of all ages enjoy contra dancing—a local tradition similar to square dancing, but with couples facing each other in rows. "It's a lot of fun," says Bunchie Angell, who joined a contra dance group in her sixties. "I have some aches and pains, and I just get there and enjoy it so much!"

Vermont is also an important center for crafts such as woodworking, weaving, pottery, and glassblowing. Many artists are inspired by old traditions. Jeanne Brink makes baskets the way her Abenaki grandmother did long ago, weaving them out of thin strips of wood and grasses. She learned from an older basket maker who asked her to promise to keep the craft within the Abenaki people. "I will only teach Abenaki how to make ash-splint and sweet grass baskets," says Brink, "to keep it an Abenaki tradition."

People have been making quilts in Vermont since before the American Revolution. A quilter might stitch hundreds of different colored pieces of cloth together to form a pattern or picture. Eliza Greenhoe-Bergh, who lives in Dummerston, makes quilts that look like paintings of the Vermont country-side. More traditional quilts are often all one color but covered with tiny stitches in a delicate design. Quilts that are 200 years old can be found in the Shelburne Museum near Burlington. Historian Richard Cleveland sees them as pieces of the state's past. "Sometimes when I find a quilt I especially like," he says,

"I run the tips of my fingers gently over its surface, willing it to tell me its secrets." Quilters from the state and from around the country come to Northfield every June or July. At that time, the town hosts the Vermont Quilt Festival. Many claim that it is New England's oldest and largest annual quilt event.

*A weaver sits by her loom at a craft center in Middlebury.*

# Make a Tin-Punch Lantern

Since the 1700s, yankee tinsmiths have made useful household items such as trays, candleholders, cookie cutters, cookware, and teapots. They also made punched tin tiles to decorate ceilings, pie cupboards, and lanterns. Follow these instructions to make your own decorative and useful tin-punch lantern.

## What You Need

An empty can with a paper label
Scissors
Marker
Water
Thick towel
Hammer
Awl or large nail
Votive candle (If you would prefer not to use candles, you can buy the battery-powered lights used in jack o' lanterns on Halloween.)
Copper wire, about 10 inches to 12 inches long
Wire cutter
Pliers
Sand (approximately 1 cup)

*You must prepare the can in advance. Be careful of any sharp edges on the rim of the can. You can have an adult help you file down the sharp edges on the rim. Wash the empty can and remove the label. Fill the can with water nearly to the top and put it in the freezer for several hours. Once the water is frozen, use the marker to draw on the can. You can draw shapes, a design, or a random pattern.*

*Find a sturdy work surface such as a table, workbench, or concrete floor. Fold a towel and place the can on it to keep it from slipping while you work. Have an adult help you set the awl or large nail along your drawings. Gently tap the awl or nail with the hammer. You do not have to drive the nail in too deep. The awl or nail will punch through to the ice. Punch holes along the rest of your design. Make two larger holes near the top of the can, opposite from each other. These holes will be used for the handle.*

*Place the can in a sink, tub, or bucket and wait for the ice to melt enough to remove it from the can. Once the can is empty, thread one end of the wire through one of the handle holes and wrap it around itself to make it secure. Use the pliers to squeeze the end of the wire so that no sharp ends are sticking out. Next, wrap the middle portion of the wire loosely around a pencil or pen to make a spiral handle. Thread the wire through the other hole and wrap it around to secure the loop, using the pliers to squeeze the end.*

*Fill the bottom of the can with about 1 inch of sand. Place the candle inside. Have an adult light the candle so that you can watch your lantern glow!*

**WARNING:** You should never light matches or candles without adult supervision. Make sure your lantern is far away from papers, walls, or anything flammable. Be careful when handling the lantern because the metal can become very hot. Never leave your lit lantern unattended.

One Vermont group, the Bread and Puppet Theater, took a very old art form and made it into something new. The artists in the group create puppets of all sizes, including figures that tower eight feet high. They put on colorful shows using the puppets along with musicians and dancers. Sometimes they get the audience to join in, and they carry a political message each time they perform. The Bread and Puppet Theater travels most of the year. In summer the group presents free outdoor shows on a farm near Glover.

*Every summer, the Bread and Puppet Theater's performances draw large crowds to Glover.*

## Heading Outdoors

One thing nearly all Vermonters have in common is their love for the outdoors. In summer they may head for the Green Mountains to camp, hike, or take a dip in a sparkling lake or clear flowing stream. Almost two-thirds of Vermonters say they like to watch wildlife. That number is more than in any other state.

Fishing is popular even in winter, when lakes and rivers are iced over. The temperature might be below zero, but the reward

*Young Vermonters learn about ice fishing at Lake Shaftsbury State Park in southwestern Vermont.*

could be a hefty lake trout, walleye, or northern pike—or just good company. "Ice fishing is a big event," says Ludolphe LaBounty of Barton. "I like to come out here and meet people. But as far as catching the fish, that [isn't] the biggest point."

Winter is also time for skiing, snowboarding, and snow-mobiling. "Skiing in Vermont is great, because there are so many places to choose from," says Karen de Seve, who grew up near Bennington. "But you have to know how to handle icy slopes and bitter cold days."

A Vermont farmer named Wilson Bentley helped show the world the amazing patterns snow crystals make. Bentley took the first close-up photograph of a snowflake in 1885. "I found that snowflakes were miracles of beauty," he wrote. "Every crystal was a masterpiece of design and no one design was ever repeated."

Even though Vermont is a beautiful state, everyone who lives there has to face icy winters, muddy springs, and roller-coaster weather. That might be one reason people like to argue about what it takes to be a "real" Vermonter. Some say it means having great-grandparents who were born in the state. To others, it means sticking with the place through thick and thin, even if you come from someplace else. "I'm not one of those who says you've got to be born here to be a Vermonter," says Graham Newell, a former state senator whose family has lived in Vermont for seven generations. "If you are a Vermonter, you feel like one and you don't have to explain it."

*A family enjoys a quick hike through the snowy fields of Greensboro.*

# Calendar of Events

## Stowe Winter Carnival

At this January festival, kids can play snow volleyball, watch an ice-carving contest, or join a race through the woods on cross-country skis.

## U.S. Open Snowboarding Championships in Stratton

Snowboarders from around the world become acrobats at this action-packed event in March. Visitors crowd around the halfpipe to watch their daredevil twists and turns.

## Vermont Maple Festival in St. Albans

Every spring, buckets of sap flow from sugar maple trees to make maple syrup. St. Albans celebrates the harvest in April with maple exhibits, a talent contest, a pancake breakfast, and a big parade.

## Abenaki Heritage Celebration in Swanton

Native Americans from Vermont and around North America come together to dance, make music, and share traditional food and crafts toward the end of May.

## Vermont Dairy Festival in Enosburg Falls

The dairy cow is the center of this farm festival in June. Visitors can pet prizewinning cows, watch a milking contest, or tap their toes to live country music.

## Vermont History Expo

In June the Vermont Historical Society presents this event at the World's Fair Grounds in Tunbridge. Highlights include historical exhibits, a parade, performances, craft displays, auctions, and many other fun activities.

*Tunbridge World's Fair*

## Ethan Allen Days in Sunderland

Music and food from Vermont's early days are some of the highlights of this June celebration. Visitors travel back in time as history fans act out battles from the Revolutionary War.

## Burlington Latino Festival

Each August, Vermont's biggest city throws a fiesta with music, food, and dancing from Mexico, Cuba, Central America, and Puerto Rico.

## Bondville Fair in Winhall

This fair is almost as old as the state of Vermont, and it has not changed much over the years. People come every August to eat fried dough, play horseshoes, and see how much weight a team of oxen can pull.

## New World Festival in Randolph

Each September, Vermonters celebrate their British and French Canadian roots with a day of old-time music, dancing, and storytelling.

## Plymouth Cheese and Harvest Festival in Plymouth Notch

This harvest celebration takes place at the family home of President Calvin Coolidge. Visitors can see what it's like to sheer a sheep, do traditional crafts, and play games at home on a farm.

## Vermont Apple Festival and Craft Show in Springfield

This October event offers a taste of country life in the Connecticut River valley, with folk music, a craft contest, and plenty of crisp, ripe apples.

*A balloon festival in Stowe*

# 4 How It Works

Ever since the time of the Green Mountain Boys, people have been working together to shape Vermont's future. Citizens may come from different backgrounds, but when they speak out and share their ideas, they often find common ground. Families all over the state need basic things like roads, schools, parks, and police departments. To support them, the people of Vermont—from private citizens to government leaders—work as a team.

## Town Meetings

Close to home, Vermont gives citizens a great way to make their voices heard: the town meeting. Everyone who lives in Vermont is a citizen of a town or a city. In some cases, several small villages or large farms all belong to one town. Most towns hold a meeting every year on the first Tuesday in March. Anyone who is old enough to vote can join in.

At town meetings, citizens elect officials, approve budgets, and pass laws. They can also speak out if they disagree with a decision or want to suggest a new one. The town meeting is a

*The Stafford Meeting House. Throughout the state's history, many Vermont communities have held their town meetings at the local meeting house.*

New England tradition that goes back to the 1700s. It is often called the purest form of democracy we know.

Vermont's state motto is "Freedom and Unity," created by Ira Allen in 1777. Even today the motto represents Vermonters' devotion to balancing the rights of individuals with the good of the community.

## At the Capital

Vermont's capital, Montpelier, is the smallest state capital in the nation. Only about 8,000 people live there, and most of its businesses fit on one main street. But its tiny size may be a good thing. It is an easy place for ordinary citizens to meet lawmakers face to face.

The Vermont legislature is known as the general assembly, which includes two parts, or houses—a house of representatives and a senate. Its members work together to make the state's laws, but anyone with an idea for a law can start the process. The first step is to write a bill—a kind of suggestion for the law—and ask a legislator to support it. The legislator can introduce the bill to the house of representatives or senate.

After a bill is introduced, it goes to a committee for discussion. Sometimes the committee holds a public hearing, where anyone can come and say what he or she thinks of the bill. The committee may reject the bill or support it. They may also decide to change, or amend, parts of it. When the committee decides the bill is ready, it gets read before the whole house or senate. That is when all members debate the bill and take a vote. Once a bill passes in one house of the general assembly, it goes to the other, where all these steps have to be repeated. A bill often goes through a lot of changes before the general assembly is done with it.

Finally, the bill lands on the governor's desk. If the governor signs it, the bill becomes law. But he or she can also reject,

*State legislators meet at the Vermont State House in Montpelier.*

or veto, a bill. Then it only becomes law if two-thirds of both houses vote for it. Making laws takes patience. Each year, about 500 bills are introduced to the general assembly. About one out of three gets signed into law.

# Branches of Government

**Executive** The governor of Vermont leads the state by seeking ideas to improve areas such as the economy, health, education, and transportation. He or she can propose laws or reject them. The governor is elected to a two-year term.

**Legislative** Vermont's legislature, the general assembly, is made up of the senate and the house of representatives. The senate has 30 members, each one representing one or more counties. The house has 150 members, representing about 3,500 citizens each. All lawmakers are elected to serve for two years. The legislature meets to hammer out new laws between January and late spring. Many lawmakers also have other jobs, such as running a business, teaching school, or farming.

**Judicial** Vermont's highest court is the supreme court, headed by a chief justice and four associate justices. The supreme court mainly hears appeals of cases decided in lower courts. They include the superior court, for civil cases such as lawsuits, and the district court, for criminal cases. Vermont also has more specialized courts such as the family court for divorce and child support, probate court for wills, and environmental court for land use disputes.

Vermont may seem old-fashioned at times, but it has made some very bold laws, especially on protecting the environment. In 1968 Vermont became the first state to outlaw billboards. In 1970 it passed Act 250, the first statewide land use law in America. This law says that before a new construction project can begin, a committee must review it with the environment in mind. One thing that makes the law special is that regular citizens make up the committees. So the people of Vermont can decide for themselves when to put limits on how land is used.

In 2000 Vermont passed another law that was the first of its kind in the nation. Known as the civil union law, it lets two men or two women form a bond, sharing many of the same rights as married (man-woman) couples. Lawmakers listened to many people and worked on the bill for months before then-governor Howard Dean signed it into law. Laws such as these cause much controversy and are a hot topic around the country today.

> *Vermont is my birthright. People there are happy and content. They belong to themselves, live within their income, and fear no man.*
> —United States president Calvin Coolidge

## Who Pays for Schools?

One challenge Vermont lawmakers face is the divide between rich towns and poor towns. The state's richest communities—called "gold towns"—include skiing centers like Stratton and Stowe. Most people in gold towns have more money and property than citizens in the rest of the state. For a long time, gold towns also had much wealthier public schools. That was because most of the money to run schools came right from the towns themselves—from local property taxes.

In 1997 Vermont tried to make the school system fairer with a new law called the Equal Education Opportunity Act, or Act 60. Under this law, residents pay property taxes to the state instead of the town. The money from this tax is shared across the state, and every school district gets about $5,000 a year for each student.

When the new law went into effect, it was a welcome break for low-income towns, because it meant more money for schools. The gold towns objected to the law. As a result of the law, many gold towns had to pay higher taxes and cut school budgets. "It's a disaster, an absolute disaster," says one fourth-grade teacher in Dorset. But Diane Wolk of the state school board disagreed. "What they're going through now is what 90 percent of towns have gone through for years and years—having to make choices," she said.

Like most laws, Act 60 is a compromise. Lawmakers have changed it more than once since it first passed. Finding ways to support education equally—and to divide the tax burden fairly—will always be a big part of the government's job.

*Education is an important issue for many Vermonters. These students are arriving at their school in the western town of Shoreham.*

## Taking a Stand

Even if you are not old enough to vote, you can still have an effect on Vermont politics. One of the best ways is to let others know your ideas. If you live in Vermont and want to support a cause, find out everything you can about the issue by going to the library, listening to the news on the radio, reading the newspaper, or using the Internet. Then write a letter to your state senator or representative explaining your point of view. If you can show that you understand all sides of an issue and have good reasons for your opinion, leaders will listen, whether you are eight years old or eighty.

Students at some Vermont schools actually do get to vote at election time. They often go to the polls with their parents. While the adults use official ballots, the students fill out ballots of their own. These mock (pretend) ballots get counted separately from the others, and the results are posted on the Vermont government Web site. Students' votes may not decide who gets to be president or governor, but when kids go to the polls, it can make a difference. Students are able to see that their votes have concrete results. Many hope that programs like these will encourage students to vote once they reach the legal age.

Others also feel that if the children are excited about voting, then their parents might also vote more often. When St. Albans students started voting in 2000, about 17 percent more adults voted, too.

**If you are interested in contacting Vermont's state legislators go to this Web site: http://www.leg.state.vt.us/legdir/legdir2.htm. It has different links you can click on to find contact information for the state's senators and representatives.**

Sometimes, just connecting with people around you can make a big difference. Students at one elementary school in Westford went door to door to find out what their neighbors did for a living. Like many farming areas in Vermont, their community was made up of many small businesses, from making maple syrup to designing pages for the Internet. The students wrote about what they learned and created a Web site about the project. By sharing their information, the students helped business owners, who had been working on their own, get to know each other. Bringing neighbors together like this can help communities thrive.

# 5 Making a Living

Vermont's fresh air, clear water, and stunning scenery make it a great place to live, but finding a job there can sometimes be challenging. Fortunately, the Vermont economy has strengths in many areas, so if there is a slump in one industry, things can pick up in another. Some people say the economy sits on a three-legged stool, made of manufacturing, agriculture, and tourism.

## Manufacturing and Mining

Most of Vermont's manufacturing jobs are located near Burlington. Companies in the area make computer chips, software, batteries, and semiconductor equipment—parts needed for all kinds of electronic items, from video games to cell phones. With its miles of forests, Vermont is also a center for wood and paper products. Saw mills produce lumber, cabinet-makers build furniture, and printing presses turn out newspapers and business forms. Some companies in the state make equipment for outdoor sports, including snowboards, snowshoes, and fishing rods.

*A young Vermonter picks corn on his family's farm in Rochester.*

Vermont also has a long history of making machine tools—the precise gadgets used by factories. Some of the first tools for shaping wood and metal by machine were invented in the 1840s in Windsor. In the beginning, these tools were used in the state to make guns, typewriters, and sewing machines. Today, machine tools made in Vermont help produce paper, steel, cars, and airplanes in factories across the country.

Windsor is home to the American Precision Museum. The museum is devoted to honoring the importance and effect of machine tools in Vermont's—and the country's—history. The nation's largest collection of historically important machine tools can be found at the museum.

The country's first granite quarry lies just outside Barre, on the eastern side the Green Mountains. Workers cut big blocks of the rock and haul them to workshops called granite sheds. Some chunks of Vermont granite are carved and polished to make

*A quarry provides shale for Vermont and other states. Shale is a type of rock used mostly in construction.*

memorial stones. Others are sliced to make the walls of office buildings or cut up to make kitchen counters.

Vermont's marble belt runs through the Taconic Mountains, in the southwestern part of the state. For more than one hundred years, stonecutters in Proctor have been shaping marble columns and graceful monuments. Today, most of this gleaming white stone is ground into a fine powder called calcium carbonate. It is then used to make toothpaste, paint, and plastics.

The United Nations Building in New York City is made from Vermont marble. So are the U.S. Supreme Court Building and the Jefferson Memorial in Washington, D.C.

## Living from the Land

Green fields, big red barns, and black-and-white cows are a familiar sight in Vermont. They are also a big part of the state's economy. About 1,400 dairy farms can be found in Vermont. More than half of these farms blanket the Champlain Valley. Some of these farms have been around for more than 200 years, with the oldest dating back to the American Revolution. Vermont has fewer dairy farms now than it did in the past, but they still play an important role. More than 11,000 people who live in the state work in jobs connected to the dairy industry.

*Dairy farms in Vermont still play an important role in the state's economy.*

Vermont dairy farms produce more than 2.6 billion pounds of milk a year. More than half of it is shipped to other states, and another 5 percent is sold locally for drinking. The rest goes to make dairy products such as yogurt, butter, ice cream, and more than fifteen kinds of cheese, especially cheddar and mozzarella.

Vermont farmers also make a living growing fruits and vegetables, such as apples and potatoes, as well as crops for animal feed, such as corn, hay, oats, and wheat. Some farmers use greenhouses to raise warm-weather vegetables like green peppers and tomatoes.

About 2,000 farmers earn money from a famous Vermont crop: the sweet sap of the sugar maple tree. People tap the trees by driving a metal spout in the trunk and letting the sap drip into a metal bucket. Then they boil it down to make syrup or mouth-watering maple sugar candy.

*A farmer harvests corn on his farm. Many Vermonters grow sweet corn and field corn.*

# Recipe for Maple Oatmeal Cookies

Here is a simple recipe for tasty cookies made with oatmeal and sweet maple syrup.

## Ingredients:
1/4 teaspoon salt
2 teaspoons baking powder
1-1/4 cup uncooked oatmeal (quick oats)
1/2 cup shortening
1 egg
1/4 cup chopped nuts (pecans or walnuts)
1 cup maple syrup
1/2 teaspoon vanilla extract
1/4 cup milk
1-1/4 cup flour

Have an adult help you preheat the oven to 350 degrees Fahrenheit.

Combine all the ingredients together in a large mixing bowl. Make sure that the batter is mixed very well. (With the help of an adult, you can use an electric mixer—set on medium speed—if you have one available.)

Lightly grease a cookie sheet. To make each cookie, drop about 1 tablespoon of dough on the cookie sheet. Make sure that there is at least 1-1/2 inches between each cookie.

Bake the cookies for about 10 minutes. The cookies should be a light brown color. Carefully remove the cookies and let them cool down. An adult should help you with this since the cookie sheet and the baked cookies will be very hot.

Once the cookies are cool, grab a glass of milk and enjoy!

*Vermonts parks, forests, and mountains are popular spots for hikers and campers.*

## Tourism

Millions of visitors travel to Vermont each year, adding about 4 billion dollars to the state's economy. In summer, people come to hike and camp in untamed areas like the Green Mountain National Forest, and to swim, fish, and canoe in sparkling rivers and lakes. In autumn, thousands of tourists arrive to catch a glimpse of the brilliant fall leaves. Winter brings skiers to mountain resorts like Stowe, Killington, and Sugarbush.

Tourists help keep the economy running by staying at hotels, eating in restaurants, and shopping in stores. In addition, many people from outside Vermont have vacation homes in the state. These part-time Vermonters not only buy property, they also pay taxes, giving the state a big financial boost.

The outdoors may be Vermont's main tourist attraction, but history and the arts bring people to the state, too. The Shelburne Museum, just south of Burlington, is one of the state's cultural treasures. The museum is not just one building, but almost fifty, spread out in a huge park full of green lawns and bright flowers. Many of the buildings are more than a century old, including a schoolhouse from 1840 and an inn from 1783. Inside them is one of the largest collections of arts and crafts from America's past.

*A young visitor learns about shipbuilding at a maritime museum in Basin Harbor near Lake Champlain.*

# Products & Resources

### Dairy Farms

About 160,000 dairy cows produce milk in Vermont. The most common type of cow in Vermont are black-and-white Holsteins. These cows can provide more than six gallons of milk a day.

### Apples

Vermont has almost 4,000 acres of commercially grown apple orchards. The bushels of crisp, tart fruit they produce are either sold fresh or made into special treats like cider, applesauce, and pie.

### Granite

Some of the world's finest granite comes from quarries near Barre, where the stone is an important part of the economy. Vermont ships this heavy building material across the United States and to many other countries.

## Electronics

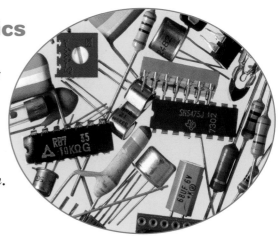

The production of electronic equipment is Vermont's leading manufacturing industry. The state's biggest private employer is International Business Machines (IBM), which runs a microchip factory near Burlington.

## Forests

The acres of trees that carpet Vermont are used to make everything from lumber to paper to maple syrup. Their fiery fall color brings income to the state by attracting thousands of tourists.

## Mountains and Snow

Vermont's mountains are a major resource for the tourism industry, attracting hikers, campers, and sightseers. In winter, the snow-covered peaks become a playground for skiing, snowboarding, and snowmobiling.

## Saving Vermont Farms

Many visitors like to come to Vermont for its simple pleasures. Tourists can drive along a narrow, winding road, pass a 200-year-old covered bridge, buy fresh fruit from a farmer, and then putter around in a country store. Most Vermonters agree the state will be better off if it keeps its old-fashioned charm. That means protecting the land and preserving historic places. It also means holding onto an important part of the rural way of life: Vermont's farms.

*Farming is your identity. It's not a nine to five job. It's in your blood and who you are.*
—Vermont farmer Beth Kennett

Farming has never really been an easy job, but it has gotten even harder over the past few years. Milk prices can drop so low that dairy farmers earn less money than they pay for feed, equipment, and property taxes. People who run small farms have an especially hard time. If they cannot make ends meet, they may wind up selling their farms to developers—people who want the land to build houses or businesses.

Most farmers would rather keep their land, and many others want them to keep it too. "Vermont wouldn't be Vermont without its farmers," says Pam Allen, who grows apples on an old family farm in South Hero. "People here don't want to see parking lots and high-rises. There is no other sight in the world like these apple trees exploding with sweet white blossoms each spring."

Vermonters are doing their best to keep small farms running. One dairy farmers' group is raising money to start a new milk bottling plant. They want to bottle their own top-quality

*Residents of farm communities—such as this one in Peacham—continue to preserve the farming tradition for which Vermont is famous.*

milk and sell it at a higher price for more income. Many others are switching to organic farming. That way they can raise prices, because people who drink organic milk and eat organic fruits and vegetables are usually willing to pay more for the special food. Farmers also get extra income by running inns for tourists or selling specialty foods like gourmet mushrooms and homestyle jam.

Conservation groups are helping too. The Vermont Land Trust, for example, pays money to farmers who agree to protect their land from development. Since the group got started in the 1970s, it has saved more than 400,000 acres in the state, including 400 working farms. Another organization, the Conservation Law Foundation, is working with the state government to get help for farmers, including tax relief, business advice, and programs to promote products that are grown close to home. One such program, called Vermont Fresh Network, links farmers to restaurants interested in buying their crops.

Farms contribute more than 500 million dollars a year to the Vermont economy. They also create the green rolling pastures Vermont is famous for. Thanks to this beautiful countryside, Vermont can be a wonderful state to visit or settle down in. And Vermonters are working hard to make sure it stays that way.

Vermont's flag was adopted in 1923. It displays the state's coat-of-arms against a blue background. The coat-of-arms includes a shield with symbols of the state's forests and farms: a pine tree, a cow, bales of hay, and stacks of wheat, with the Green Mountains in the background. The head of a stag—a male deer—is at the top of the shield, and pine branches curve around it. The name of the state and the Vermont motto, "Freedom and Unity," are written on a red banner underneath.

The state seal was created by an early settler named Ira Allen. Like his brother Ethan Allen, Ira helped Vermont become a state. The seal was originally adopted in 1779. It shows the state motto below a pine tree, a cow, sheaves of grain, and wooded hills. A newer version was introduced in 1821, but Vermonters decided to use the original design. In 1937 Ira Allen's design once again became the official seal.

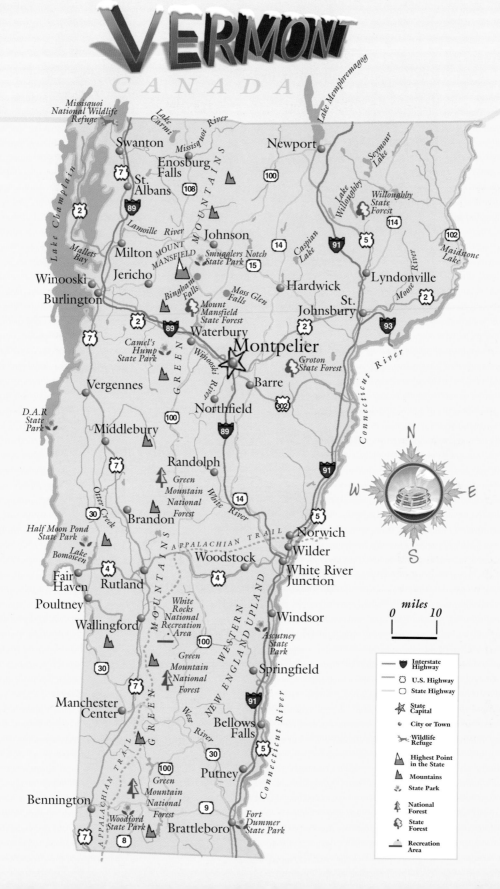

# VERMONT

## CANADA

Missisquoi National Wildlife Refuge

Swanton

Enosburg Falls

Newport

Lake Memphremagog

Lake Carmi

Missisquoi River

Seymour Lake

7

St. Albans

108

100

Lake Willoughby

Willoughby State Forest

89

Lamoille River

MOUNT MANSFIELD

Johnson

14

91

5

114

Milton

Smugglers Notch State Park

15

Caspian Lake

102

Maidstone Lake

Lake Champlain

Jericho

Bingham Falls

Moss Glen Falls

Hardwick

Lyndonville

Winooski

Burlington

Mallets Bay

Mount Mansfield State Forest

Moose River

2

2

89

Waterbury

St. Johnsbury

93

Camel's Hump State Park

GREEN

Winooski River

Montpelier

Groton State Forest

7

Vergennes

Barre

302

D.A.R State Park

100

Northfield

89

Middlebury

Randolph

Green Mountain National Forest

White River

14

5

Brandon

Otter Creek

APPALACHIAN TRAIL

Norwich

Wilder

Half Moon Pond State Park

Lake Bomoseen

Woodstock

White River Junction

30

4

Fair Haven

Rutland

4

White Rocks National Recreation Area

WESTERN

Windsor

Poultney

Ascutney State Park

Wallingford

100

Green Mountain National Forest

NEW ENGLAND UPLAND

Springfield

30

91

7

GREEN

West River

5

Manchester Center

MOUNTAINS

Connecticut River

Bellows Falls

30

100

APPALACHIAN TRAIL

9

Putney

Green Mountain National Forest

Bennington

Woodford State Park

Brattleboro

Fort Dummer State Park

7

8

### Legend

- ━ Interstate Highway
- U.S. Highway
- State Highway
- ★ State Capital
- • City or Town
- Wildlife Refuge
- ▲ Highest Point in the State
- ▲ Mountains
- State Park
- National Forest
- State Forest
- Recreation Area

miles
0     10

N
W    E
S

# Hail Vermont!

## Words and music by
## Josephine Hovey Perry

CHORUS

# More About Vermont

## Books

Czech, Jan M. *Vermont.* New York: Children's Press, 2002.

Feeney, Kathy. *Vermont Facts and Symbols.* Mankato, MN: Capstone Press, 2003.

Flocker, Michael. *Vermont: The Green Mountain State.* Milwaukee, WI: World Almanac Library, 2002.

Henry, Marguerite. *Justin Morgan Had a Horse.* New York: Macmillan (Aladdin Books), 1991.

Stein, R. Conrad. *Ethan Allen and the Green Mountain Boys.* New York: Children's Press, 2003.

## Web Sites

**Official Portal of Vermont:**

Vermont.gov

**Official Vermont Tourism Site:**

www.travel-vermont.com

**Vermont Fish and Wildlife Department:**

www.vtfishandwildlife.com

**Vermont's Secretary of State Web page for kids:**

www.sec.state.vt.us/Kids

## About the Author

Margaret Dornfeld is a writer, editor, and translator in New York City. She loves painting, cooking, and listening to Latin music. On summer days, she likes to escape the city and go canoeing in the lakes and rivers of Vermont.

# Index

Page numbers in **boldface** are illustrations.